Tell me about Jesus

By Elizabeth E. Watson

Illustrated by Don Kueker and Assoc.

D1728123

CONCORDIA®

Publishing House

St. Louis

TELL ME ABOUT JESUS

Copyright © 1980 by Concordia Publishing House
3558 South Jefferson Avenue, St. Louis, MO 63118

ISBN: 0-570-03484-1
Printed in the United States of America

3 4 5 6 7 8 9 10 11   WW   90 89 88 87 86 85 84 83

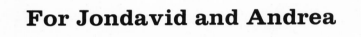

For Jondavid and Andrea

Tell me about Jesus. Oh, won't you, please!

Tell me how He came to earth as a baby.
Tell me how He was born in a stable,
in the town of Bethlehem.
I know! Mary was His mother.

I love to hear how the angels sang
the night of His birth.
Tell me about the shepherds who came
to worship the Baby in the manger.
Tell me, please, about the Wise Men
who came from the east.
They followed the star and brought gifts
to give to the Child Jesus.
I love to hear the story.
Tell me about Jesus.
Oh, please just one more time.

Tell me how He grew up in the town
of Nazareth and became a carpenter.
Is that why people called Him
Jesus of Nazareth?
Jesus learned and worshiped in the temple
when He was a boy.
Tell me what He did when He grew up to be a man.
I love to hear that story.

Tell me how He was baptized by John the Baptizer.
Tell me how He went into the desert all alone
to be tempted by the devil.
Oh, please tell me the way Jesus was perfect
and never did anything wrong.

Tell me how Jesus selected His disciples.
I'll try to remember them.
Tell me about Peter, the big strong fisherman.
Tell me about James and John, the brothers.
Tell me about Matthew, the tax collector
who decided to follow Jesus.
Tell me about poor doubting Thomas.
Tell me about . . .

Yes, and if you have to, you can tell me about
Judas.

Tell me more about Jesus.
Tell me about the wonderful things He did.
Tell me how He walked on the water.
And how He calmed the wind and the waves
in the storm.

Tell me how He made sick people well,
blind people see, and lame people walk.
Tell me how He fed 5,000 people
with only five loaves of bread
and two little fish.
Tell me how He even raised Lazarus from the dead!

Tell me about Jesus, just once more!
Tell me some of the things He said.
Tell me how He taught on the mountainside
and by the seashore.
Tell me how He taught us to love God
and one another.

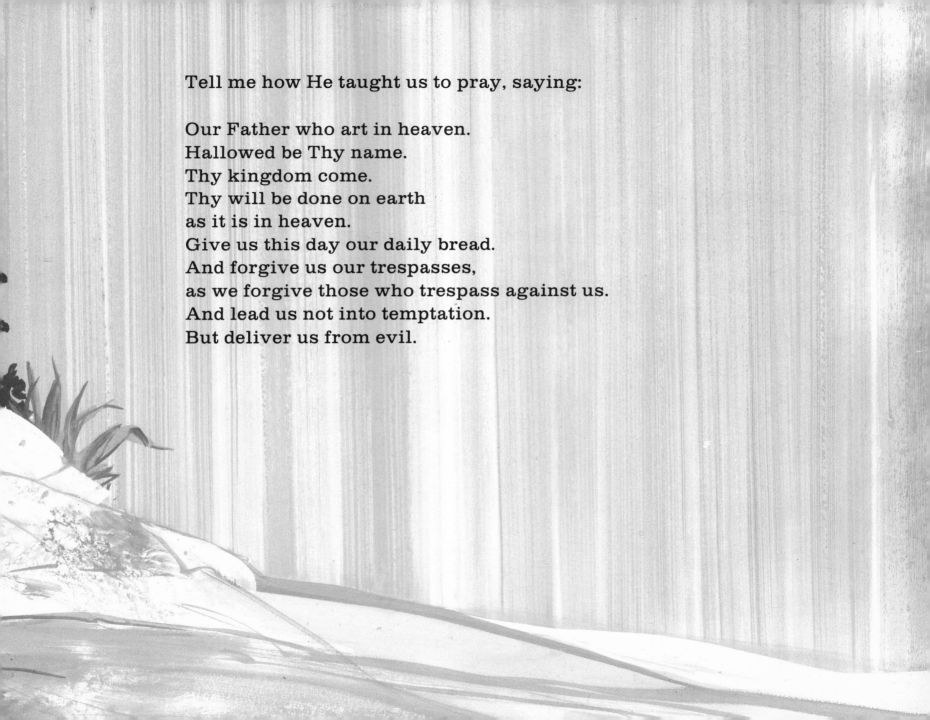

Tell me how He taught us to pray, saying:

Our Father who art in heaven.
Hallowed be Thy name.
Thy kingdom come.
Thy will be done on earth
as it is in heaven.
Give us this day our daily bread.
And forgive us our trespasses,
as we forgive those who trespass against us.
And lead us not into temptation.
But deliver us from evil.

Tell me some of the stories He told.
I know. They are called parables.
Tell me how the boy's father was happy
when his son came home again.
Tell me how God our heavenly Father is happy
when sinners come back to Him.
Tell me how He forgives them like a loving father.

Tell me how Jesus died for our sins.
I'll try not to cry.
Tell me how one day He suffered
and died on a horrible cross . . .
just for us.
Tell me how on the third day
He arose from the tomb . . .
He was alive again!

Tell me how Jesus is alive today.
I love to be told about Jesus.
Tell me that Jesus is God's only Son.
Tell me how God sent His Son Jesus
to die in our place.
Tell me how Jesus died for me,
so I can live in heaven with God.
Jesus is with me.

I like to hear how He watches
over me each day, when I am awake
and when I am asleep.
I like to hear that He forgives me
when I do something wrong
and I tell Him I am sorry.

Tell me how Jesus wants me
to love Him.
Oh, I do, I do.
You don't have to tell me that.

I know that for sure!